A   esign

Edited by Sarah and Mariam Moore

First published by East Winter Books
an imprint of Thought and Company Ltd,
13 Sunbury Workshops, Swanfield Street, London E2 7LF
www.eastwinter.com

The publisher makes no representation, express or implied, with
regard to the accuracy of the information contained in this book
and cannot accept any legal responsibility or liability for any
errors or omissions that may be made.

Set in Garamond Premier Pro AgfaRotis and Roboto

ISBN: 978-0-9935046-0-0

Contents

Acknowledgements

I wish to acknowledge the help that a number of people have given me during the course of this project.
To begin with I would like to express my thanks to Maria Cheung and Paul Westmoreland along with Gregory Epps for their support, and for critical motivation Aureliusz Kowalczyk, Simon Gazzard, Avni Patel, Josef Huber, Jennifer Mensah, Alison Crawshaw and Ella Chau. Finally Libin Chen and Wei Liu for their input on distribution.

Sound judgement and no little skill has been exercised by Sarah and Mariam Moore in their editorial surgery and general recovery efforts.

Image Credits:

Pages 64-65:
Image of object 1971.603 Marshall Islands Chart. Image courtesy of the Horniman Museum and Gardens care of the HORNIMAN MUSEUM AND GARDENS 100 London Road, Forest Hill, London, SE23 3PQ

Page 93:
100 Chairs in 100 days, London 2007
Designed by: Martino Gamper   www.martinogamper.com
Photograph: © Angus Mill   www.angus-mill.com

Page 94:
Koloro-desk, Tokyo 2012
Designed by: Torafu Architects
Photograph: © Akihiro Ito

www.torafu.com
www.a-110.com

Page 95:
Cine Lidia, Tarragona 2003
Architects: David Tapias and Nuria Salvado
Photograph: © José Hevia

www.aixopluc.net
www.josehevia.es

Page 96:
K-Space, London 2008
Designed by: 6a Architects
Photography: © David Grandorge

www.6a.co.uk
www.grandorge.com

Page 97:
AM3: Andreas Murkudis Store, Berlin 2004
Designed by: GONZALEZ HAASE AAS
Photograph: © Thomas Meyer - Ostkreuz

www.gonzalezhaase.com
www.thomas-meyer.com

Page 98:
Rauch House, Schlins 2008
Designed by: Roger Boltshauser & Martin Rauch,
Rammed Earth by Lehm Ton Erde Baukunst GmbH,
Ceramic tiles by KARAK - Marta & Sebastian Rauch
www.lehmtonerde.at/de/martin-rauch
Photograph: © Beat Bühler

www.beatbuehler.ch

Page 99:
The Petri Church, Klippan 1966
Architect: Sigurd Lewerentz, 1885 - 1975
Photograph: © Josep Maria Torra

www.flickr.com/photos/jmtp/

Page 100:
Hof Residence, Malmeyjarfjordhur 2007
Architects: Studio Granda
Photograph: © Sigurgeir Sigurjönsson

www.studiogranda.is

A preface

Whether your intentions are clear or uncertain, this text aims to meditate on an approach to the design of interiors moving towards an *interior architecture*.

Interior architecture (generally called interior design) is positioned somewhere between furniture and architecture. It encompasses much more than the selection finishes and fittings. This text aims to consider some of the thought processes involved in translating a brief into a design proposal. How your decision-making strategies and interests develop throughout your design career.

Written with London in mind, a city with centuries of built history and a current population of 8.6 million over 1,575 square kilometres. A city where land for construction is increasingly difficult to find*, implying a natural increase in interior refurbishment projects of every type – requiring more considered interior architecture.

Within the text boundaries with other creative disciplines are intentionally imprecise. We aim to wander between fashion, storytelling, architecture, cookery and furniture – but always with an intention to build on a theoretical (and pragmatic) approach to the interior design process.

In more immediate terms this is a partial introduction based around six chapters, not all of which will make sense

---

* It is worth noting London is less dense than many other world cities such as Mumbai, Shanghai, Paris, Istanbul.. www.citymayors.com/statistics

initially – in fact, some might never, the first chapter is a light preamble on the notion of trends in design and the idea of quality.

In a dramatic twist, chapter two attempts to provide an overview of a design process in eight moves and has three substantial sections. At first this might appear to be a daunting list of items to think about but try not to be dissuaded, as with most things worth doing if you intend to produce work of substance enough to attract other people's attention then it's worth understanding some of the many approaches towards designing interiors available to you for adaptation. In time and with practice the list still won't get any shorter but instead you'll improve, intuition will begin to take over, decisions will start to make more sense – with practice.

From within this chapter three of the eight moves are focused on and discussed in more depth in proceeding sub-chapters: Sketch modelling, Diagramming, Collage.

The remaining chapters take a careful rock climb through various highly debatable opinions and thoughts on the design process. Considering questions you might want to incorporate as part of your own way of working, while compiling the puzzle pieces generated by research and design. The text eventually concludes with a sample of a studio design brief intended for further experimentation. Though in reality, of these last chapters the selected reading list is probably the most significant.

4

00_Introduction

Within many professional circles and public opinion the division between interior design and architecture is clear. In practice these two disciplines are often conducted at different stages, and in many cases are required to cater to different clients.

However (and in principle) both practices share an interest in the built environment, both attempt to engage with light and the idea of 'Place', both occasionally often overlap in responsibilities and both share common elements such as doors, windows, ceilings, floors and stairs.

For reasons of scale, complexity and cost, Architecture is widely regarded as carrying the greater responsibility, where Interior Design tends to play the part of the fashionable younger sibling. However, I would like to focus on the interior, its importance and the idea of meaning.

A thought for the relevance of the interior – as compared to the exterior, though the two are not mutually exclusive.

Try to imagine a time line, representing days, weeks or hours of your time spent either at work, in the library, or at home. Consider the proportion of time you might typically spend within this building, as a guest of its interior. Finally, review this against the proportion of time you might spend 'looking at' this same building. The difference between the two should be clear therefore the relevance of the interior (as opposed to the exterior) also becomes clear.

According to EU research on air pollution it is believed that we spend 85% – 90% of our adult lives indoors (climate dependant), approximately 6% of the remaining time spent in some form of vehicle travelling - from one interior to another. Even assuming a reasonable factor for the time spent indoors looking outwards at neighbouring buildings, the overall ratio still doesn't quite explain the lack of emphasis (in the Architectural media) on interior design.

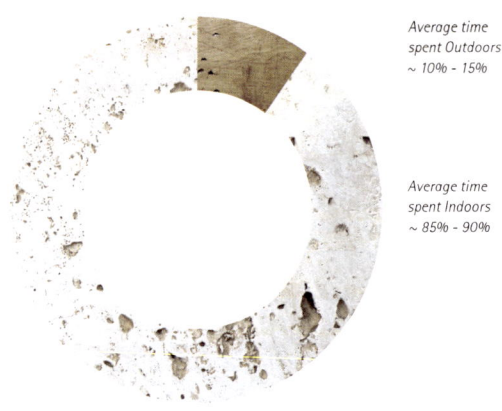

Average time spent Outdoors ~ 10% - 15%

Average time spent Indoors ~ 85% - 90%

A lifetime inside: Comparison of time spent within buildings as compared to time outside. Summary of data obtained from the UK Office of National Statistics and EC Air Pollution Research IP/03/1278. Brussels, 2003

Where common design media critique and understanding of new projects are concerned this can be a potential issue; representation of the exterior of a project often outweighs imagery and discussion of its interior. In this way the experience of 'being' in, moving around and using a building is also difficult to effectively represent in the context of an article or photographic series. This hypothesis is largely based on an impression of the ratios of exterior to interior photography of new architecture projects in recent archives of many popular online design blogs such as Dezeen.com and Designboom.com.

To consider a more holistic impact of the interior on physical health, work, life, and emotional well-being (all in proportion) there lies the potential to create the foundations of environments and places. Places that could in time come to represent different meanings for those of us fortunate enough to occupy them.

Many interior design students have at some point expressed an understanding of the practice of Interior Design as being in some way easier than or largely subordinate to the practice of Architecture. There are situations or moments where it could be argued that this is true, but for the most part and depending on their field of practice Interior designers have an alternate set of responsibilities and in many cases greater scope for creative input – as hopefully revealed in the earlier meditation on indoor time.

If your primary interests stop at the surface qualities of interior design, this text might not be of use. The aim and interest here is to provide another path towards imagining places with qualities difficult to capture in renderings or photographs alone, but easy to appreciate as environments of value – even if only for one occupant. A deeper interest in emotional response.

This is attempted with an understanding that we learn differently, where some gain more from experimentation trial-and-error and experience, others benefit from a more theoretical understanding and structured academic study. In most cases this is more of a sliding scale between empirical and theoretical on which you might find yourself at different points for different subject types at different stages of your education. Further adjusted by proximity to other recently learned subjects. It is hoped that, eventually, you will have experienced each position along the scale, before deciding on a position or two that best intuitively suit your own ways of doing.

By nature of this being a text it exists at the theoretical end of this sliding scale, yet ultimately it is in fact focussed on the empirical (learning by doing) end. Through design attempts, through sketching collaging and model making, through seeking feedback and re-iterations of these stages, you should acquire a stronger array of design skills and a more individual theoretical perspective. A process of application, adaptation and growth.

After all, there is normally much less risk involved in a design critique or studio review of a hypothetical project than the financial and emotional risks involved in a built project. It might be useful to think of your education as a head start before the core responsibilities of professional practice begin. As a comment on 'risk' an appendix to this introduction would be 'The role of the mistake'.

Therefore, please continue on the understanding that, until the thoughts conveyed from here on have been tested within your own design projects their value may be limited.

Common perceptions of the interior design process often relate to filmic stereotypes, featuring a designer of some sort conjuring an abstract concept or similar novelty based idea, before leading into illustrations and mood boards perhaps followed up by realistic computer renderings presented to eager clients. Indeed, this is not entirely uncommon. There are many ways in which this method has been successful and in many other respects this is a method that doesn't really need to be taught in the traditional sense. That is to say for many the appearance of skill can be largely approximated through enough exposure to Interior Design magazines, blogs, TV shows and media. After all, if a client doesn't know any better, isn't expecting anything beyond the sense of 'luxury' or the economic pragmatism of a corporate environment – with a token splash of colour, then where is the need for deeper understanding – why try harder?

Instead, the interest here is in the continued development of your ability as a designer, skill as a craftsperson and ultimately through these your standards as a practitioner. In this respect your design output will begin to acquire its own integrity and you should eventually come to see the notion of imitating others or cutting corners as unacceptable.

> 'Isaac Stern rule: the better your technique, the more impossible your standards.'
> *Richard Sennett, The Craftsman*

A few of the benefits of traditional educational frameworks are:

a. An understanding of a skill as the application of a craft which comes through various elements of practical experience. Whether conjuring ideas and understanding the material consequences costs and workmanship required, or presenting them to clients and contractors, along with good mentoring, these elements are difficult to substitute.

b. The creative adaptation of a design scenario, the designers 'talent' for want of a better word.

c. The considered application of a methodology, a way of doing. Where balance is attained through the consideration of the project's audience in its entirety: the client, the media, the staff who'll be spending over forty hours a week there, the visitors, and the maintenance staff engaged in looking after it. Some designers like to change methods from project to project, and some develop and refine the one. In either case with enough practice a level of experience is obtained whereby this component merges with [a] and almost disappears as a conscious activity.

d.   Personal development with a like minded peer group. Possibly the most important of the points and unfortunately many schools forget to state this. From a longer term career perspective a committed student peer group provides healthy competition and mutual support while potentially forming your first professional network. Though it's beyond the scope of this text it is something worth thinking about if you're in a position to find others in a similar situation.

These entities are not mutually exclusive, and engaged constructively each should reinforce the other. At any one point in time you might feel unable to focus on more than one or sometimes two of these, however, given time and practice all four will converge into a singular more robust skill set. It is this cocktail with its discrete ratios that are often referred to when individual design 'masters' are name-checked.

This text is intended to support tutorials and aims to address the third (methodology / ways of doing) of these four aspects with indications of where the second (talent) might be introduced.

For the remainder of this discourse, and perhaps for education as a whole, larger subjects are subdivided into smaller components for the sake of communication, but really it is hoped that they will eventually reconfigure themselves into an individually adapted way of working (modus operandi) through your own practice and perseverance.

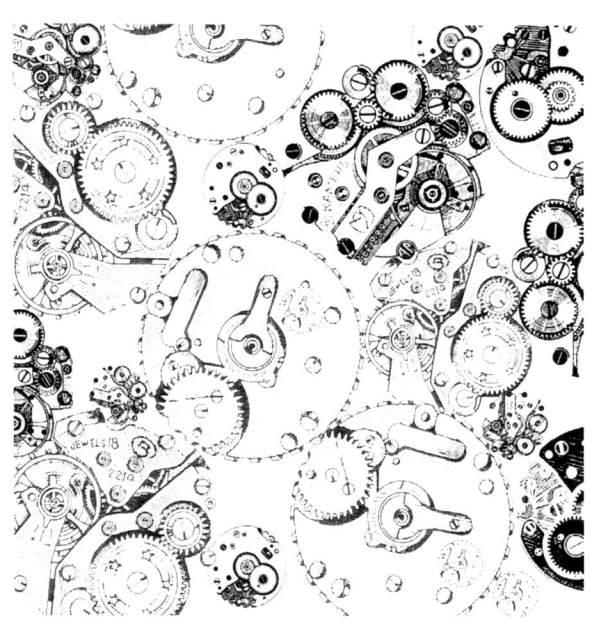

*Epps, Gregory 2000, Device for scaring poltergeists', Digital [Detail]
Concept for a clockwork flooring tile to automate and animate
furniture layouts.*

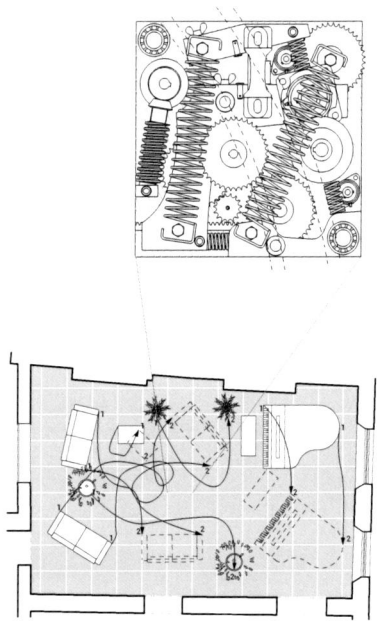

*Epps, Gregory 2000, Device for scaring poltergeists', Digital [Plan]
Concept for a clockwork flooring tile to automate and animate
furniture layouts.*

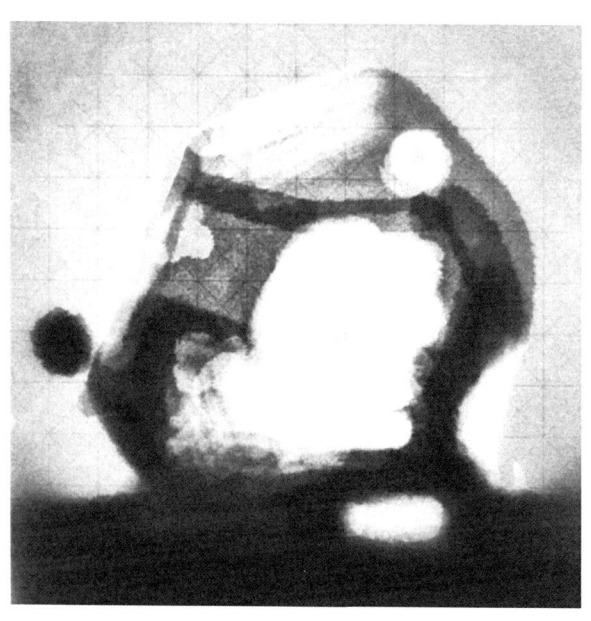

Lekker, Arthur 2014, Cross-section, Digital sketch.
A notional exploration the relationship between interior and
architectural space

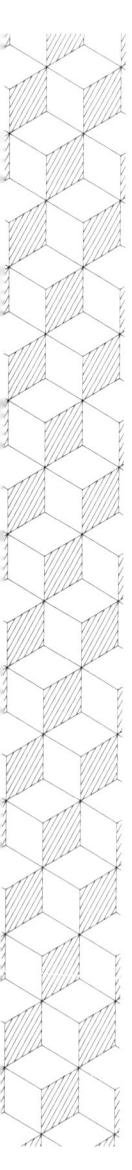

18

01_Design trends, design quality

'There are many architects who aren't really aware of their own patterns, just like most people don't know their patterns in private. We find that a really exciting theme because architecture and psychology suddenly become very close.'
Jacques Herzog

In Herzog's statement, as elsewhere in this text, the word 'patterns' is used to describe working or thinking habits. 'behaviour patterns'. These patterns are neither good or bad in themselves but if recognised and used effectively they can be slowly tweaked to improve the deeper, more intuitive, levels of the ways in which we see and approach design.

Connections have been made by various thinkers in the past between the way we arrange our interior minds and the way we organise our physical surroundings, hectic thoughts are reflected in chaotic private spaces. The number of 'things' and visual elements per square meter (the density of 'stuff') can make a direct appeal to how we might be expected to feel about a place; ranging from the intentionally calm, visually restrained white wall 'minimalist' spaces of many contemporary art galleries, to the graphically busy object rich environments of delicatessens, bohemian coffee shops and maybe your own living room. The visually calm interior with its almost spiritual allusions and the jumbled casual appearance of a homely interior can both be relaxing, but in interestingly different ways. If one could be said to speak of a tranquil calm, the other of a form of socialised comfort, then where do the many interiors you might sample on a walk across town sit in this range of density? How do these different densities correlate to different atmospheres, and how close does each arrangement, each design, each style, come to achieving its intended state of mind?

> 'If a cluttered desk is a sign of a cluttered mind, of what, then, is an empty desk a sign?'
> *Albert Einstein*

The portfolio works of many designers could be said to be definable by particular 'identity'. Considering the view they've acquired from many years of practice based experience these identities and their names often become associated with particular types of formal expression. In this respect individual designers are often brought to mind when projects of a particular or distinctive style are presented, due in part to typical constraints of representation many such styles have come to be canonized by their formal motifs. Or put more simply; different languages of form become branded by different designers, and in this way the shape of a building might be easily recognisable as a 'Zaha Hadid', or a 'Verner Panton'.

Consider also that sibling disciplines (typography, film making, fashion, the fine arts, product design, and the like) typically have their own primary forms of representation (mediums) in which they can fully express their intentions. For example; the discipline of photography has the photograph, to write or sing about photography may on occasion also provide effective means to communicate the essence of a particular photographic project but ultimately the message is best communicated through the photograph. The same could also be said for fashion through clothing and the feel of fabric, filmmaking through film, writing through text, sculpture through form and so on.

Unfortunately, with the exception of branded retail interiors, it is very difficult to effectively transport or mass-duplicate good works of interior design. Interior design is harder to contain effectively in any one form of representation because it is about the combined experience of place, time, material, light.

To return to the earlier rumination on recognisable identity, it is very easy for this idea of a primary interior medium (the first hand spatial experience) to be overpowered by the designers formal motifs – as these elements tend to be easier to photograph. Therefore, in developing an understanding of interior design, over reliance on project articles risks limiting your potential to create more substantial interior moments.

Though some forms of atmosphere can be captured in photographs film or in text, there are other more immediate atmospheric experiences achievable through successful Interior Design that can only be experienced first hand by visiting the original project. In this way it is clear that Interior Design is a very site specific practice. There are of course exceptions to most rules but the consequence of this is, at least in the process of learning about designed space, that it is very important that texts and images be taken as second hand information and that ultimate judgements and tangible understandings of any given project are withheld until such places have been visited and experienced first hand – wherever possible. As an analogy; you might read an enticing article on a particular dish or a well written recipe, description of its flavours, and a series of very convincing food photographs, as perhaps on Instagram, but no matter how good it looks it is not quite the same as actually tasting it.

In this media arena the recognisable brandable form tends to acquire momentum within the design press. And there is a tendency for young designers to take on board the photographs' imagery and consequent notions of shape making as a level of practice to aspire to. Indeed, to all intents and purposes, this is the often rewarded approach - where being published is the de facto form of recognition and achievement. However, to do only this might be akin to reconstructing a Michelin star meal from a photograph and a brief description and hoping this alone will improve your skills as a chef. Instead, and to repeat, the message here is to review the blog article book chapter or magazine spread and then aspire to visiting the place in question (where possible) in person before reaching any final conclusions.

As noted this practice of stylistic formalism lends itself to publication but for a designer (as 'brand') to maintain this and 'make a name for his or herself' sometimes means repeating the same formal motifs across all projects. Failing to do so may be considered inconsistent and may elicit criticism from the very media that lauded their work originally. Equally, criticism is sometimes levied when the same technique is applied repetitively to projects that would better suit an adapted, localised approach. Altogether this means that to practice with a recognisable 'brand' could be understood as both strength and constraining weakness.

As a counterbalance the broader your experience, the wider your understanding of other designer's approaches and the more experimental your application during the small span of time between education and developing a formal position of your own (be it intentional or not), the potentially more flexible and thus robust your approach to design might become.

This is all based on the idea of the 'designer as abstract artist' imposing a method upon a programme or specific project whether appropriate or not, which has ethical implications. Though it is important to acknowledge this as a real thread in practice this text seeks to develop an understanding of a design process in which occupants (those who use the building), programme, and context are prioritised above and before the expression of a particular form.

That said, it would be difficult to discuss the education of an interior designer without making some assertions, and so feel free to take and critique the examples referred to here as a representation of this writer's current interests, note that in most cases the examples are selected for specific instances of decision making and coordinated thinking, with which it is hoped you'll be able to see beyond trends and reflect design considerations beyond any one position of style.

'Space', is one of the most commonly used words during the design phase of architecture and interior design – for many students starting out a word that can take a little time to dissociate from its astrological references. By comparison, '*place*' is less commonly used but (I would like to propose) equally important word.

Many interiors are not designed to last indefinitely, shop 'fit-outs' and many other types of brand oriented interior for example are rarely designed with more than a few years in mind, as new product trends are anticipated and tenancies tend to be on short leases. To borrow a term from another industry, this is sometimes referred to as 'planned obsolescence' where a product is designed to be redundant after a limited period of time. Arguably this is a core part of the business model for many interior design practices aiming for repeat work, though it should be considered; with each redundancy the next commission is theoretically available to any other design company.

> 'When one is writing a letter, he should think that the recipient will make it into a hanging scroll.'
>
> *Tsunetomo Yamamoto, Hagakure:*
> *The Book of the Samurai*

It's difficult to predict how a work will be interpreted by those who experience it, so consider that even temporary projects may invoke lasting memories.

Thus in both temporary and permanent cases it is worth aiming for design quality, either to develop something robust, enough to attract other clients attention or to help a client choose to reuse you for the project's next stage. Above all to create a memorable place where light, material, function and form are well balanced in context.

In these two scenarios (temporary or permanent) this robustness of design quality refers to a consistency of thought and action. Design quality here refers to a scheme or a designers attempts to consider alternative approaches, including and exploring input from other disciplines, while extracting as much information as possible from the brief. Ultimately the more details you have within a brief the more specific and thus tailored your output can

become, this is where we find opportunities to increase a project's depth. Design quality here contains the extra considerations and thoughts gleaned from research into the subject matter behind a given interior.
Research into the history of the existing building, materials, suitable techniques, the given project's subject matter, and research into similar projects which have successfully combined the first two strands of research into a coherent and well composed internal environment.

And so, the design decisions you choose to make next should begin to feel and look more informed, resulting in a sense of designed-in (built-in) quality.

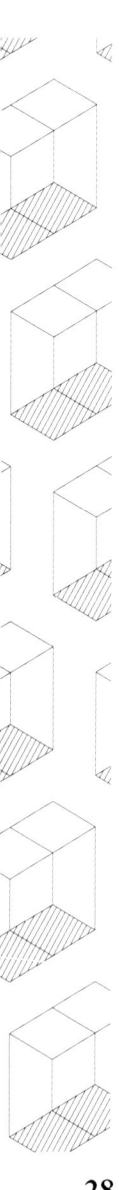

02_Approaches, process and play

There are many methods and approaches available to you during the process of developing a design and further means for ultimately achieving physical space just as there are many different ways to prepare a meal. In all cases these methods exist to narrow the field and focus on a path within a constantly changing sea of possibilities, thus making the potentially daunting task of designing and constructing more manageable.

As a backdrop, many designers prefer to adopt a 'problem solving' view where design briefs and user needs are labelled as 'problems' – to be solved by a design 'solution'. This perspective helps to objectify and distance the sometimes complex requirements of a design brief, which in turn makes it theoretically easier to reduce a larger problem down into a series of smaller problems that are easier to tackle. The terms 'method' 'technique' 'approach' 'system' mentioned above are all words that fit into the rational pattern of a 'problem-solution' design approach.

However, an alternative to the 'problem-solution' design approach can be found in some of the patterns of thought more commonly adopted by the fine arts, musicians, therapists, tailors and, to be fair, those practitioners within Interior Design who are experienced enough to see positive opportunities beyond a brief.

Where it is easy to objectify a designed object as a conscious 'solution' it is perhaps less common for us (as consumers ourselves) to think about and consciously objectify our needs as 'problems'. In this sense a 'want' for something, a 'desire' for something, or a 'need' is rarely the same as a sudoku, a riddle, or a mathematical 'problem'. We could view design briefs as opportunities, situations of interest, subjects to explore, or simply people seeking delight.

Though the first pattern – that of the problem seeking mind – is quite popular it's really the second pattern of thought we aim for here, with both together we can begin to reach a level of balance. Einstein's expression 'Play is the highest form of research' sits well in its ability to relate the desire-seeking yet often educational process of 'Play' to the more analytical often solution oriented process of 'research'.

This balance is difficult to achieve. It is very easy for a designer or project to come across as whimsical self indulgent or overly superficial if the core mechanics of its brief remain unresolved. On the other hand it is equally possible for the outcome of an entirely rational design process, where all of the requirements of a brief have been methodically resolved, to feel impersonal or another kind of empty.

Now with this in mind we'll consider the highly adaptive problem solving approaches at play in a design process.

To begin with, we'll take the process of cooking a meal as an active analogy. If we consider for a moment the basic stages of preparing a dish we have many possible methods at our disposal in:

- **Preparing** – peeling, chopping, grating, slicing, blending, whisking, soaking and so on
- **Cooking** – frying, toasting, poaching, boiling, grilling, steaming, baking, mashing et al, while balancing timings
- **Presenting** – dressings, arranging, the bringing together of the various ingredients (where not already combined) and the last 'plated' presentation

This is a sequence of options that could in many ways parallel with baking a design:

Preparing (research) – interviewing, photographing, writing, material-sampling, precedents, web surveying and others

Cooking – sketching, modelling(sketch) photographing, writing, diagramming, drawing, collage-making, tracing et al, while researching as needed.

Presenting – image formatting, typography, printing, narrating, the bringing together of the various media into a composed, narrated arrangement.

Just as a wide range of recognisable dishes might be prepared through the outlined three cooking stages, an equally wide range of design outcomes are developed through the design stages described above. This is where the element of play enters the process. Just as with cooking, it's possible to circulate within and between the first two stages. For example, we could grille something before then toasting it in a sandwich or adding it to a soup, and then baking in some form of casserole which might then taste terrible ...or fantastic? And so to adapt this analogy, this flexibility is possible in a design process where in most cases the more we iterate within the cooking stage and chain together different methods the more potentially delicious ...or terrible the design output.

Each of these iterations effects a change to the drawing, image or model you're developing. Each change provides a kind of feedback through small realisations (for example an initial sketch model of a waiting room interior might reveal that seats are actually too far apart for families to sit together where other configurations are better for couples or individuals, and maybe the ceiling feels too high) giving you the option to make further adjustments in response. In this manner we are able to converse with a project as it matures into something more interesting. As with cooking the more we practice and experiment with each method the greater our understanding of how and where best to deploy each.

These design cooking stages relate to a process of development. Which is largely distinct from the brief and the problem-solving/desire-seeking strands of what we do.

Where:

- ○ **Brief** equals – what we need want and desire. The research and food prep [an understanding of what's involved to create the required dish - something lunch sized that's a little spicy, not-too-heavy, nutritious].
- ○ **Process** equals – how we're going to go about making it: which to chop/dice/slice/mash and which pots to cook with and which methods to grill it under.
- ○ '**Desire-Solution**' equals – what we're making, the nature of the dish itself: air fried whole grain rice balls with a salsa dip (!?)

In the case of our waiting room sketch model the first ingredient, for a Citizens Advice Bureau we should consider the view a visitor will have upon entering the room. This view influences how long they might feel comfortable waiting. A small (phone) camera to take (and print!) a few key photo's from within our sketch model. Using tracing paper we can then sketch over these images to better imagine how compose a less intimidating more relaxing scene, one where a visitor can quickly assess the best place to sit – without having to endure too many curious gazes others.

This new messy sketch is the next ingredient. We can simply use another sheet to trace out the more desirable lines for a clearer scene. Next we morph it into a collage by adding cut outs of scanned materials, textures from a preselected palette, remember: we're still playing, so the textures do not have to be to scale! This material play might then whisk into the furniture play where we start to experience how the furniture materials, forms and colours and associated colours start to taste when folded into the rest of the interior material palette. Now we have a better understanding of what is more or less important to us in the space, we can communicate this with a quick sketch diagram to illustrate the key interests.

The oven is now preheated and we can return to our sketch model with improved direction to cut, glue, add, bend, taste, subtract to better align it to the sketch collages. Once again the model has priority (though perhaps not for materials) and it should be re-evaluated from various angles before making further adjustments. Re-fry and repeat the photography and collage rounds as necessary to develop and form a cohesive space, perhaps slightly varying the material palette, perhaps adding screens, tall furniture or large plants to create subtle privacy where needed but still keeping a clear view of all seats from the receptionists desk - spatial relationships which should be noted in a further diagram. With enough practice, iteration and the play of changing between media will become more fluid and intuitive.

With a suitably baked sketch model you should now be able to 'plate it up' by using it to help you draw up (or reiterate) the plan of the space and one or two key sections as orthogonal scale drawings. The model will also provide the basis for a final set of views which again can be collaged and traced into for a reinforced array of graphics conveying the design intentions thus assembling the main course of a presentation.

This is just a taster of a very model oriented process for a single interior space to help demonstrate how the vital relationship between development making and drawing. This illustrates how by prioritising design play in one type of media can help expand other types as the project progresses.

There are, as already mentioned as many different design processes as there are methods to prepare food. Initial practice in one will enhance your ability to take on others.

Equally, there are as many different variations of a design process as there are designs. The following chapter aims to break down a typical example of a design process as a sequence of eight moves each with their own respective processes based around three 'w's leading from a design brief, to a design proposal. Here we will list and outline the steps within this sequence before expanding on each point.

1.   *Understanding:*

> 'One very important aspect of motivation is
> the willingness to stop and to look at things
> that no one else has bothered to look at. This
> simple process of focusing on things that are
> normally taken for granted is a powerful
> source of creativity.'
>   *Edward de Bono*

> 'Designing is a matter of concentration. You
> go deep into what you want to do. It's about
> intensive research, really. The concentration
> is warm and intimate and like the fire inside
> the earth – intense but not distorted. You
> can go to a place, really feel it in your heart.
> It's actually a beautiful feeling.'
>   *Peter Zumthor*

a.   '**who**' – who owns and who will occupy
      – who is the client,
b.   '**where**' – the history of the site, of the client, and
      the general context of the project,
c.   '**what**' – the programme or purpose, many would
      describe this as the function.

'Understanding' – possibly the most important design
stage, the importance of this can not be stressed enough.
The aim is to achieve a deep understanding of the
individuals or people who dwell in work in or visit the

space you'll be designing, as for the history and nature of the existing building and locality, this will build into the quality of your design thinking and eventual proposal. For many this begins as a data gathering exercise, accruing information in various formats, and in the case of good detective work it is important to avoid making assumptions or taking any knowledge for granted. The 'who', the 'where' and the 'what' will each generate a wealth of information, most of which may not have a clear purpose initially. Most of that won't need further presentation, however, further interrogation of the output may begin to reveal deeper links, hidden connections between programme, place history, neighbouring activities that should help to add intensity relevance and depth to your emerging proposal. From here on out these three 'w's form the core of our reference when we use the term 'Research'.

The start of a design process: Research

To be clear, this is not the stage to seek out or invent a grand concept or singular design principle. Though, should one or more occur to you while investigating, sketch it out and keep it for a later stage. Ideally, this research stage should focus on learning more about the context of the design brief, because eventually a solid understanding of the real background and hidden layers of your client, your site and your programme will increase your credibility as author and add to your experience as a designer.

At first this might seem to be an abstract task, and you may ask why we are not yet designing? Well, if you look around at all the interior spaces in any given city or social context which have no or very little 'quality' about them, such interiors have little or no atmosphere or feeling: the 'plastic' highly commercialised spaces, where the new inside has little or no bond with its outside – or anything else of interest. Forgettable places you probably wouldn't choose to spend any more time than was absolutely necessary. These are environments with very little character where the extent of design thought applied is reduced to the selection of products from a catalogue, yet is somehow presented as 'interior design'.

If you're observant, you may occasionally happen upon interior spaces full of atmosphere and intention, some simple, some elaborate, either designed by considerate designers or unintentionally 'designed' by people without design backgrounds or design aspirations – places sometimes referred to as 'honest' or 'vernacular' – and these spaces are often more interesting and significant than any of the unconsidered, 'designed' interiors which are light on character.

After cooking, a second analogy would be the Bespoke tailor (or Dressmaker). Take a moment to imagine hiring a professional to produce for you a very expensive outfit for a specific occasion. Typically you might at least expect this person to find out from you what kind of occasion the garment is intended for and would probably expect to be measured for a fitting. These are the most basic of tailoring questions, and without these it would be highly likely that the resulting suit or dress would fit or be appropriate for its occasion. In the arena of interior design these and more sophisticated research questions should be addressed.

Your own investigative questions and research should (eventually) move beyond found 'reference' images and web-found text. Providing you can find links of critical interest there should be decisions about materials (moving beyond the generic 'wood' or 'metal' but instead specifying particular species or treatments, such as; 'fumed oak' or 'petrolised brass' for example) and then colour configurations or approaches to lighting and how these can be combined to create the space you are imagining.

Other research material should enable you to describe the full constellation of your subject, returning to the three 'w's in turn to;

○ discuss and reflect the means by which the audience within your scheme interacts with one another – the other 'who's,

○ illustrate the stages and processes involved in the 'what's of your programme (perhaps through diagrams),

○ consider the interaction and meaning of this project in the context of its surroundings – the 'where's,

○ and, ultimately, how your various discoveries start to interconnect and weave together.

If you've found any, you should start to unearth your inspirations towards the end of this first stage – if not then you should allow yourself space and time for new ideas to appear.

It is important to remember there are a wide range of interior types, beyond the usual coffee shops, office interiors, and private apartments, available for development. Places you've probably seen or passed through in the past without very much thought, ranging from airport check-in and departure lounges to bus and train station waiting areas, from hospital waiting areas and patient wards, to schools and university staff areas, student areas, theatres and their lobbies, research laboratories, music recording studios, tailors workshops, nurseries, museums, vehicle cabins, gyms, launderettes, cooking schools, virtual environments, and so on.

Design thinking in each of these various types cross pollinates, so that understanding acquired from dealing with the specifics of one situation can often provide creative solutions to design opportunities presented in another. For example, lessons learnt in how to provide perfect ventilation in research laboratories may later lead into more effective cooking school designs; experience gained from designing components in museum interiors coupled with nursery design moves to engage children could cross over into hospital waiting room interiors or family areas of airport departure lounges. Experience and cross pollination. Again, balance is important, balance between cross-disciplinary design and specialisation – it's quite possible for some to spend a career specialising in one type of 'what' and still evolve an equally strong skill set based purely on an ability to master one position incredibly well.

It is not uncommon for Architects to think about the design of a project in stages starting from the macro scale to the micro, gradually moving from outside and into the interior, before then reiterating the process to achieve a degree of balance. Interior designers sometimes take the opposite approach, and one recommended method is to start with an object critical to the projects programme – for example if the subject is a restaurant a starting object might be the dining table, or even the spoon. These objects are (or become) key subjects, or appetizers – key subjects to instigate the research – investigating relevant types of dining, how table sizes might affect social interaction, table materials relative to the type of food to be served, moving out from the table to the chairs, to the flooring, ceiling, walls and others. Addressing the social context; the nature of interactions between waiter and diners, diners and chef, and importantly, diners and diners. Later the design proposal itself might begin with the cutlery and the table as central focus, the core concept or approach, and a means of conveying atmospheric intentions.

Understand the design purpose, who this is for, how they intend to use it, the historical background, and the built context. This research lends authority to your design decisions, validity to your work, believability to the design output. As an exercise it comes before and in between all others.

2.   *Narrative*

The beginning, middle, end of your design proposal the entrance -movement -destination within your interior project. Narrative concepts are considered in more depth in the Narrative sub section.

Briefly looking ahead at presentation narratives, and in outlining a design proposal, variations of the following pattern are often used to frame a more discursive approach: While thinking about a project for [client and purpose] ...based in [location]... initial research revealed the story of [interesting and potentially relevant fragments]... and how this lead to [something slightly more relevant]... eventually, these aspects contributed to the idea of [current design approach] ...and so forth.

3.   The diagram

A simplified reduction of a larger or more complex system, more commonly used to explain new information.

This is an important means of explaining an idea or communicating the more complex aspects of a project. For many this is a vital part of the design process.

The diagram is a useful design tool, a means of abstracting for reflecting thoughts back to yourself, without intending to be as direct or as immediate as sketching.

We will explore thoughts on diagramming in section 2b.

4.   Materials (concept) and objects

Research considering appropriate surfaces and objects. Early consideration of material types should take into account the different parameters involved in any one surface – colour, texture, type, temperature, finish. For example if you are considering 'wood' as a material for an interior this can easily be expanded to a more specific 'oak, stained grey, oiled lightly' because for any given material type there is a vocabulary of options distinguishing an appropriate 'wood' table from an unsuitable 'wood' table besides its form and detailing. This is true also for concrete, metal, glass and so on.

In addition to the materials, the coordination of all an interior project's components should be considered, even if the intention is for an uncoordinated environment. This critical approach can operate across scales, thinking about how the style and materiality of a door handle might relate to the language of the window frames, or how the lighting strategy will help define/accentuate the textures and colours selected. This approach is the backbone of a 'design strategy' and should result in the feeling of continuity and consistency of a considered Interior.

Materials also have an ontological position, that is to say a cultural and historical understanding. This is where the raw nature of some materials can be considered to be more earthly, and others (typically more processed) inherently synthetic. This plays through in their relationship to one another; it is somehow visually awkward or not quite right to place a stone top on a plastic table frame. These relationships aren't just to do with the visual weights of the materials but also the relationship to the ground where stone, marble, concrete and ceramic, materials extracted and made from the ground or earth tend to be positioned lower – as flooring or stairs. Wood, plaster, glass tend to operate mid-level as furniture walls windows, and doors. Finally painted surfaces, and even plastics are used as ceilings. This is by no means a strict rule, metals and fabrics tend to be used across all levels from top to bottom but if a higher level material is used in a lower position it usually follows that similar or higher level materials placed above it work well.

5.   *Sketch modelling*

> 'A man who works with his hands is a
> laborer; a man who works with his hands
> and his brain is a craftsman; but a man who
> works with his hands and his brain and his
> heart is an artist.'
> *Louis Nizer*

These are 'ways of doing' that work:

- as a design tool
- as a sculptural exercise
- as a way to engage directly with the three
  dimensional qualities of both form and place/space

These components of the design process are better suited
to people starting out who are perhaps less confident at
drawing. By thinking through sketch model making and
collage you should find yourself in a stronger position to
create and expand on other forms of two dimensional
representation. Further thoughts are expanded on in
Section 02d: Sketch model sculpting.

6.   *Clarifying the plan + section*

Combining the diagram and dissecting the sketch model to
develop a plan. This is the beginning of an iterative process.

7.   Critique / Review

If your critics merely nod their heads and say the work is good, then this was probably not a good Studio review/ Crit*. Reviews are not tutorials but an opportunity to theoretically test the direction and limitations of your proposal before developing further. But before all of this, interests and directions should be discussed with your design peers to spot weaknesses and opportunities before larger presentations are committed.

8.   Rinse and repeat [1 – 7]

> 'Creativity is allowing yourself
> to make mistakes. Art is knowing
> which ones to keep.'
>   *Scott Adams*

This time around ask more specific research questions to find out more useful information. Amend the diagrams and plans to better reflect the feedback and better portray the project's key intentions. Perhaps the narrative doesn't change but the collage could be edited – at this stage the pivotal views can be better identified and focused. New sketch models should be attempted, further addressing specific areas, as well as the whole. All of these facets should be developed codependently, with each step thinking of the others, not least the materiality – which should always be present as a guide. During this second revision all materials should start to become more

---

Depending on your locale:
Crit = Project critique / Project review / Studio review panel et al

specific, with clearer ideas of colour, surface finish, thicknesses and so forth, a whole host of attributes each considered to better communicate an intended look or particular interior atmosphere.

With this background body of prep work revised and developed the plans and sections should now be in a position to undergo their first revision. It is key that the revisions made take full consideration of comments from previous critiques – incorporating any recommendations alterations while keeping the core intentions clear.

Though overall this might at first seem like a long process it is important to remember that in reality these eight moves are not discrete steps, but instead phases that overlap and sometimes reappear in small quantities within each other. When one is mastered the others tend to fall into place, a flow develops and the process starts to feel less like a sequence, more like a story in the making.

You'll be able to exercise a level of judgement regarding how and where you choose to apply these design stages on a project by project basis

Error

It has been said that the only way to avoid criticism is to say nothing, do nothing and be nothing (Elbert Hubbard), and so to become a designer you'll need to make a decision as to how you respond to feedback. Some learn to deflect it, some use the defensive, others are able to adapt the worst of it to improve and develop as designers. The risk lies in placing yourself within your projects completely as you experiment and layer, whilst being agile enough to step outside on occasion to reflect on your errors and listen to the input of others – no matter how harsh or difficult it may seem at the time. In theory, if you can maintain this agility, your output will improve and critique will become conversion.

In this respect it is important to maintain a willingness to make mistakes, to enable other successes, to build experience, and ultimately develop as a designer. Errors made now are less likely to be made again later when situations might be more costly.

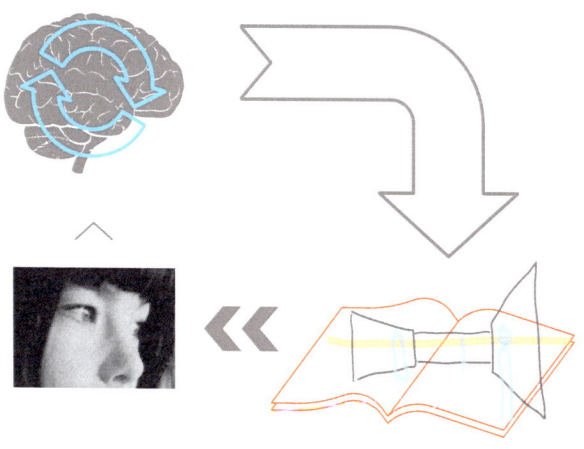

Sketching as part of an iterative design loop:
Think, sketch, rethink, sketch, thi. . . .

a_Narrative

Four key statements for those in a hurry;

1. Beginning – middle – end. Entrance – movement –
    destination. The structuring of key spaces through
    diagramming + early interior collage.
2. The sequencing of small experiences, the flow of
    movement from outside to in, public to private and
    in relation to common archetypes; residential, retail,
    office, community, cultural and so on.
3. The experience of moving from one place/space to
    another, door types and stair directions.
4. Interior design continuity between rooms and of the
    build up as one approaches a key space, perhaps increas-
    ing the use of common elements to signify change.

'Picture This' by Molly Bang discusses and walks the
reader through the anatomy of simple visual narrative,
whether that image is a photograph, a drawing or a
painting. By looking at the way in which we understand
graphic elements and the relationships between things we
label as characters on a page she describes the power and
ease of effective visual composition.

This works for the individual image as well as a structured
sequence of images focused on telling a story. For interiors
on a larger scale it should not be too difficult to see how
this approach might apply to a designed route within
a building. Typical routes for theatres, from entering

the reception area to buying a ticket at the box office, to meeting someone at the bar, to taking your seat in the auditorium. For leisure centres, from entering to changing to showering to diving into the pool, for waited restaurants, for museums, and the like.

The novel; Voyage autour de ma chambre (1794) also known as 'A Journey Around My Room (Hesperus Classics)' Xavier de Maistre expands on the possible depths of how much our imaginations can read into a single space by imaginatively weaving a travel narrative into and around a single room. Written as an autobiographical account of a fictional experience, it is also a forty two day travelogue and part vehicle for his own thoughts on life. This novel appeals to the places where we tend to spend more time than we realise, interiors and elements whose potential we often overlook.

> 'A bed sees us born, and sees us die. It is the
> ever changing scene upon which the human
> race play by turns interesting dramas,
> laughable farces, and fearful tragedies.
> It is a cradle decked with flowers.
> A throne of love. A sepulchre.' *p35*

Xavier's story developed as a result of being placed under house arrest for duelling and confined to his home. From here he took the time to really appreciate the imaginary expanse of his domain transforming a difficult situation into the opportunity of his first publication.

'[...] The pleasure to be found in travelling round one's room is sheltered from the restless jealousy of men, and is independent of Fortune.' *p27*

In thinking about this it is not a great leap to see how the smaller details of a room can have a great importance. This is especially true where and when we find ourselves confined – whether in a bedroom, a waiting room or a hospital ward. In this way too, with some imagination, it might be possible to see how narrative can be applied across a series of rooms, or when considering the walk of a gaze within a single interior.

Etching by Veyssier D, from 'A Journey Around my Room' by Xavier de Maistre 1794

The idea of a singular narrative becomes complex where a project spans multiple floors. Fewer navigation options make it easier to imagine a focussed route but in reality where fire regulations require multiple exit options and sometimes more than one stairway setting up an effective narrative is less straightforward.

When given the opportunity to design a new stair it is important to think of it as more than just a method to move between floors. Spiral stairs for example are often rotated to best suit the track of the gaze – to reveal the next space to the person using it as they rotate around it at just the right height. Other types of stair should ideally be orientated to unfold the next space in the most suitable way for your intended movement sequence.

For those thinking about the meaning of narrative and ways to build on it. Professional story artist Emma Coats tweeted a series of twenty two guideline notes on how to write a story, these were compiled on the blog page of Pixar Touch (you can find the link in the reading list) and was made to help writers create narratives. As a small example of how design approaches from one discipline might translate to interior thinking here are ten points of particular relevance to interior design thinking:

#2: You gotta keep in mind what's interesting to you as an audience, not what's fun to do as a writer. They can be v. different.

[Often within the design process the features that might be of more interest to the interior occupants those dwelling in the environment you imagine are overtaken by other sometimes less appropriate ideas, ideas that a designer was keen to try out as they were attractive as concepts, but not necessarily appropriate for the project in question.]

#3: Trying for theme is important, but you won't see what the story is actually about til you're at the end of it. Now rewrite.

[If you've already sketched out the principles of the beginning middle and end spaces imagine them together to see how they flow. Then redesign and repeat until the sequence and the idea of movement becomes more coherent. Try this process for individual interiors as for the whole project.]

#6: What is your character good at, comfortable with? Throw the polar opposite at them. Challenge them. How do they deal?

[A crude example in a design context might mean walking a visitor through a very cramped space before opening a small door directly into a very large cavernous place – spatial contrast. Better interpretations might include or play with other attributes such as lighting, colour, material along with others and all to play with (not work against) the programme.]

#7: Come up with your ending before you figure out your middle. Seriously. Endings are hard, get yours working up front.

[Start with the final (destination) interior space first, then move backwards using elements of it to help design the preceding spaces. This will help with the lead-up and weave it into the remainder of the project.]

#10: Pull apart the stories you like. What you like in them is a part of you; you've got to recognize it before you can use it.

[An ongoing exercise; reconsider and critique the places you've experienced and appreciated. These experiences often form the basis of your design vocabulary, and so from here it should be possible to recognise the importance of travel and the education of experiencing (and thinking about) as many different places as you can or are able to.]

#11: Putting it on paper lets you start fixing it. If it stays in your head, a perfect idea, you'll never share it with anyone.

[...and it will never develop. The paper of your sketchbook is a building sized workbench, where you can privately experiment with interior ideas turning one into several and sometimes questionable ideas, the good ones can later be developed into real constructs]

#12: Discount the 1st thing that comes to mind. And the 2nd, 3rd, 4th, 5th – get the obvious out of the way. Surprise yourself.

[This is often where the more interesting design thoughts start to occur, and this is where you find yourself making decisions a non-designer wouldn't normally think of, but try to keep the brief and the occupants' needs in mind.]

> #15: If you were your character, in this situation, how would you feel? Honesty lends credibility to unbelievable situations.

[For design thinking it is important to emphasise with those you imagine to be moving through your interiors, this will help you create a more engaging collection of spaces.]

> #17: No work is ever wasted. If it's not working, let go and move on - it'll come back around to be useful later.

[This requires a little self discipline and means always thinking of the occupants' needs and the programme, even whilst playing, to help determine the best way forward. You can always save the wilder ideas in your sketchbook for later projects.]

> #22: What's the essence of your story? Most economical telling of it? If you know that, you can build out from there.

[Expanding on #3, after you've designed the first draft, or the most important key space, you can build out from there' by repeating elements and expanding on others to reinforce the principle ideas. This also means editing out the less helpful or superficial elements where appropriate and exercising self restraint.]

These twenty two points by Emma Coates illustrate how film is one of the only other mediums that comes close to capturing (and playing with) some of the qualities of spatial narrative. In addition to the experiential and character led sequences described, interior design has a broader impact on the senses. An interior is an immersive typically interactive environment it is affected by the ever changing nature of daylight as it illuminates the passing of time across furniture, ventilation to manipulate smells such as synthetic freshly baked bread aroma you sometimes experience when walking into a supermarket, the changing reverb of sound bouncing from materials to let you know whether you're in a soft space or a larger hard space, the motion or stillness of airflow to let you know where the windows are open or you're standing near the facade, and so on. By understanding the potential of these and other attributes you can reinforce the possibilities of the environments you design.

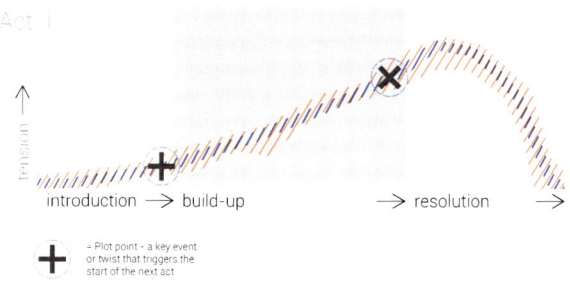

Act I

tension →

introduction ⟶ build-up   ⟶ resolution   ⟶

+ = Plot point - a key event or twist that triggers the start of the next act

Storytelling: Rise and fall tension as an emotional experience over a typical narrative sequence.

b_Diagramming

The fine art of diagramming has no set graphic language or form. Here we would like to explore the notion of the diagram as haiku, as tweet, as surgical mirror, a tool for developing an approach, something part way between a sketch and a detailed drawing. Diagrams aim to be self-explanatory and, if successful, able to represent particular project ideas not immediately clear in the plans or interior views.

In architecture and interiors 'access diagrams' have simple objectives; to communicate the way you intend to organise the elements of your project, to reflect the programme (the purpose) of your building and its narrative – how it will be 'read' by people moving through or using your final design.

This is reflected in the movement from public to private, the transition sequence from entry to the most secure/ nested part of a floor plan. How is this internal progression expressed? And as we move into a plan what happens to our attire; umbrella, hat, coat, shoes?

This idea of structuring appears in other disciplines where, for example, Filmmakers will develop storyboards describing the sequence of views and the narrative of a film as a means to focus on the key elements. This is an exercise and method for designing coherent places.

Where a plan or elevation describes – like a financial report attempts to discuss without bias, a diagram aims to explain – whether it's discussing a relationship between different components or considering one part of a complex system.

Sometimes during the early days of a project, where you find yourself struggling to formulate an approach towards a part or a whole of a project, too many possible options (or at least the illusion of such) present themselves – causing indecision and doubt. This phase is an opportunity to sketch out a few of the possibilities – leaving room for intuition to copilot and edit – before taking a focused moment to diagram the remainder. Picture a typical visitor map for a museum, a break down of a large collection of interiors for a new visitor, another form of diagram might look at a moment where windows in internal walls reveal an opportune slice of a view across an adjacent interior – or similar – tying back to some aspect of the brief, further diagrams might focus on (for example) a key factor of the entrance sequence, the way the window shutters handle and direct interior light, how the floor texture subtly transitions from one area to the next, how select tiling patterns reference different periods from local history, how the furniture collection and tone reinforce a transition from public to private rooms for an occupant – and again for a guest, and so on.

Diagramming is a visual and multidisciplinary language but can it work as a means to expand spatial design thinking while learning from other professional viewpoints? If you can keep an open mind when looking at other areas of design, especially where descriptive graphics are used you should soon start to develop your own unique vocabulary of graphic elements and means of communication.

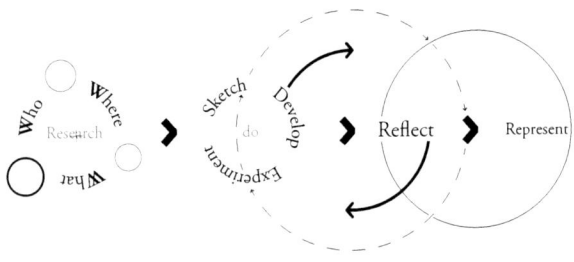

Approaches: A design process from research to representation

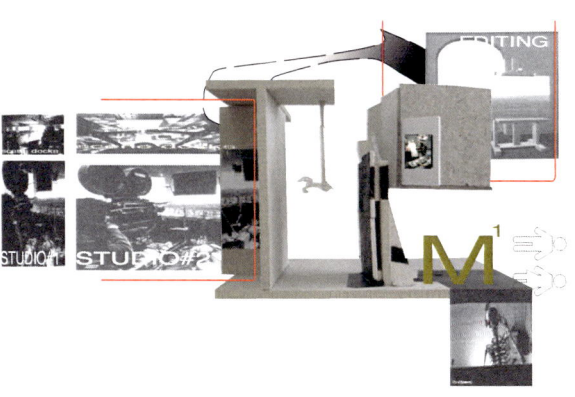

London International Film School, student design project 2000. A concept study of a corridor. Collaged Sketch model combined with Access Diagram excerpt

Public

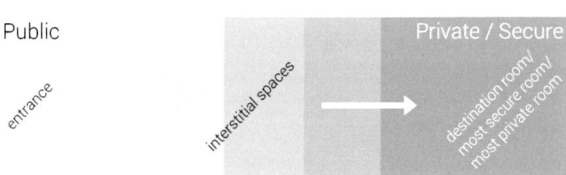

Private / Secure

entrance

interstitial spaces

destination room/
most secure room/
most private room

Typical sequence of interiors for most western buildings

Access diagrams

For larger scale interior projects, where the arrangement of rooms is within your scope, the following diagrams are an approach towards organising and composing these arrangements.

The key principle centers on the movement from Public spaces towards the Private interiors.

Here Public simply means 'most pubilc' and Private means 'most secure', in the sense that an office foyer or a domestic entrance hallway could be considered the most public of the associated interior rooms, and the CEO's office or the Bedroom could considered the most private and thus theoretically most secure.

With this in mind it should be possible to list out all of the required room types or functions for a programme and organise them along the sliding scale of the public-private axis.

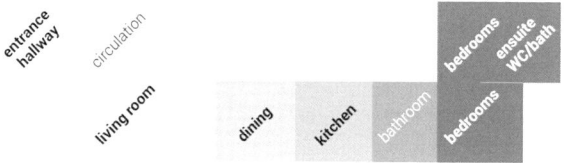

Example residential access sequence

Eventually in later versions of this method the words should be turned into graphics (indicative textures, symbols, shapes) that begin to represent the more expressive aspects of the rooms. This is because the words alone cannot proportionally represent the sizes of the spaces in question or their character.

As part of this metamorphosis the very shape of the diagram should begin to be transformed into something more akin to the available site layout. Individual relationships can be reviewed and spaces combined as necessary to help move towards a more dynamic but still function-ing plan layout. Hopefully at this point the results will look and feel like a more considered arrangement and nothing like the original access diagram sequence.

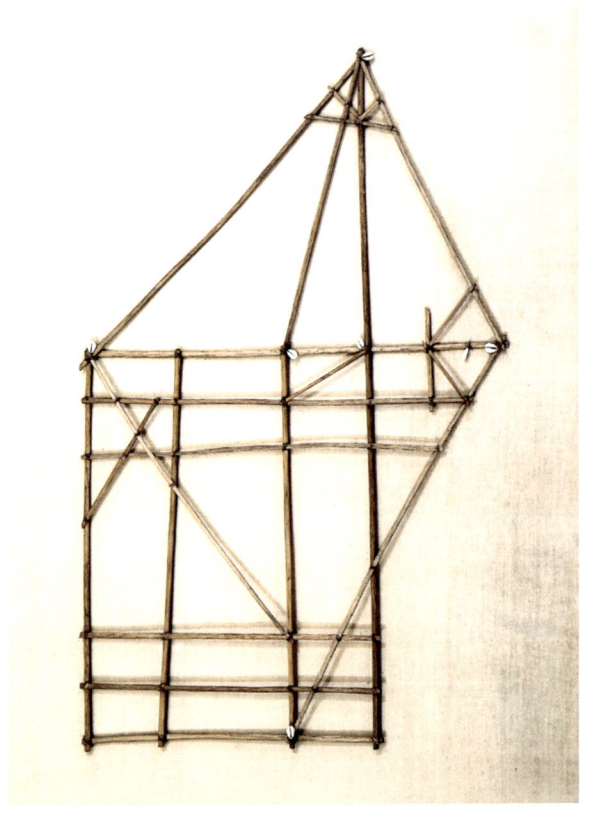

Marshall Islands Navigation Chart

object 1971.603. An entirely alternative approach to diagramming. This stick chart, made and used by fishermen, forms a useable map of the Marshall Islands and noteable water swells and currents

Marshall Islands Navigation Chart Detail

Detail of object 1971.603.. On this three dimensional diagram the shells represent islands and the angles of stick reflect the 'ebb and flow' of the surrounding seas based on the chart makers own understanding.

c_Collage

person, texture, framework, object

Within the context of a collage these are the elements of space that combine to create a sense of place. Though this constitutes another list, where you can remember to apply these words to images you see the 'list' will eventually evaporate and you should be left with a fast method to analyse understand, and then inform the composition and layering of your own images with a greater sense of depth.

Person, provides scale, a sense of inhabitation, a sense of identity (a member of the interior for a moment), and thus becomes a protagonist. However, if the person is too fashionable, or otherwise too visually interesting he/she will dominate the attention of a viewer and weaken the rest of the scene. Notice the eye line of the person being introduced and relate it to the relative eye line of the scene itself – your eyeline as the viewer should approximately align with the character(s) within the scene which should in turn relate in height to nearby vertical lines.

Texture (material), including colour, visually enriching surfaces of interest while adding compositional weight. Where applied sparingly and strategically texture brings the balance and/or a visual dynamic to a scene. Materials with the subtlest of surface structures can be as effective as heavy set textures – often even materials that appear to be plain or synthetic have landscapes of their own when observed close. In practice it's useful to build a curated folder in your computer of collected material scans.

Materials in themselves are not entirely abstract entities, they often have cultural associations, for example specific woods historically have different uses in areas of life/ industry that associate with their identity. There is often the opportunity to use your research and the brief to inform a project specific range of appropriate surfaces – a vocabulary of textures.

Colour as well as the 'weight' (visual density) of a texture have a natural order which (can) provide a sense of depth. In colour; darker surfaces and elements are placed below – while lighter components belong above. With material; older natural materials beneath sit comfortably beneath – with newer synthetic materials above. With objects; more density below (furniture and associated items) – more space above (lower density, fewer picture frames, other wall decorations).

Selecting the design of, for example, flooring; The feeling of matter beneath your soles has a direct impact on the quality and the experience of an interior. Your choice of colour, traction, solidity material and the context of the flooring possesses the greatest ability to make an impact yet is all too often overlooked.

Framework, may also include lines. This addresses the volumetric composition of space, views and formal qualities of a view. The depth and shape of an interior, the height of the ceiling, the positions of windows, stairs, doors, and other defining lines. Here interior photographs of models can provide a useful guide in the process of defining lines composing and layering elements to assemble a collage. Eventually after removing the original background photographs the remaining image should begin to stand on its own.

Object, includes furniture fixtures and fittings. Specifically positioned objects immediately allow a viewer – similar to the role of the person – to provide a sense of scale in view. Objects can also create a subtle set of relationships within a view, specific connections between 'things' where for example all objects belonging to or of a given place might be defined by the same colour, or perhaps there is only one object in each category – one chair, one wall hung picture, one coffee table and so on, and they are all of the same proportion of rectangle. Maybe each object is made from the one material but some small component of each is composed of a common material element (the legs of a chair, the top of the coffee table, the left edge of the picture frame). Perhaps a wall mounted picture contains a different pictorial composition of the same collection of objects. Such details help as internal cross references to provide (or suggest) potentially interesting design moves within an interior design.

In this way the process of collage making should be considered a useful part of the design process – not just the last step as a form of presentation. This approach allows room to play, a developed form of sketching.

Furniture also provides spatial orientation and meaning. The installation of a bed will almost always imply 'bedroom'. The position of a desk and chair in a Study in relation to other furniture, the window and the door will signify the quality of study space intended.

Furniture has the potential to define the interior – whether defining spatial roles, defining views, or providing the more pragmatic functions. It is therefore worthy of some attention – if it hasn't already been considered in the second iteration.

The highly curated interiors of Mario Praz's House of Life illustrates the bind between domestic place and the personality of the dweller (inhabitant) Professor Praz (1896 – 1982), an academic scholar, pioneered new approaches to the understanding and documentation of interior space. He rigorously adapted his personal space – enriching it with art historical and personal references. The House of Life is an experiential example of his philosophies exposed through a tour of his Rome apartment – which exists today as the Mario Praz Museum. This scholar's collection of interior elements presents layers of connected arrangements of furniture sculpture, and other objects which then reappear within some of the collected paintings. The collection may not be consistent with today's styles or contemporary tastes, nevertheless it does stand as an example of how there is often opportunity to weave layers of thought into a project whilst expanding the depths of a scene.

Object matrix. If a room is limited to three pieces of furniture what will they be, and (out of curiosity) can the same interior function as effectively with less? Like a small family tree, what's the structure of their relationship?

Lighting. As a second tier to the object matrix how does the lighting hierarchy stand. Floor-standing wall-mounted, ceiling suspended or concealed, perhaps more likely a directed combination. Which is ambient, which 'feature', and as objects do they conflict with or complement the furniture. Again, let's aim for three.

Fit-out, build as much into a space as appropriate, this is a means to integrate architecture with furniture. Through well integrated mantle-pieces shelving window seating lighting nooks deepened door frames and so on, any remaining selected furniture will be more of a feature. Moving beyond the idea of furniture.

Image dynamics:
Depth: the stacking of foreground mid-stage and background, essentially three layers. In tandem we can emphasise any contrasting light and dark areas to promote one area over another, further increasing the visual timbre.

It may not be necessary to use both layering and light-shadow contrast together as they can easily overwhelm the original intent of a collage. Applying too many 'effects' in Photoshop or 'filters' in Instagram can have a similar effect on an image, but sometimes it's necessary to go too far to understand the limits before editing back to something clearer and more effective.

Perspective: For single interior views, face on orthogonal views are generally preferable to angled or views tilted to look down or upwards. Try to avoid extreme perspective wide-angle views as they rarely do the content justice and present a false impression of space. You should always try allow the content of your view and the composition of its elements to provide the interest.

Composition: This provides the opportunity to apply a sense of character (your personal touch) to the view. Careful consideration should be made of the arrangement of furniture, the possible addition of a person for scale and narrative, the idea of the gaze and where you'd like to take it. Starting with the smallest number of graphic components the completed view will start to take shape. You may even use abstracted shapes at first to better illustrate balance, a rectangle for a window or door, or tabletop; a tall rhombus for a person, or sculpture; a larger trapezium (or two) to represent the dominant surface of the view's background be it the floor, wall(s) or ceiling. Using these shapes as a guide we can quickly review different compositions, looking at the weight depth and balance of these elements within a scene, before returning to the original backdrop and further developing the composition. Be careful when using images of people as it's very easy for the graphic of a person's appearance to distract the interest of the viewer's gaze from the designed content – especially where there's more than one person in view.

Colour, can be an awkward issue. If this is so then begin with a muted palette of one. A single tone on which to compliment and build on with another. You may find it easier to compose with hues of a single colour. Perhaps cast key interior elements in a contrasting colour to highlight aspects of your programme – where appropriate to your programme. As a rule, if there's uncertainty, try not to stray beyond three colours in an interior.

Where there's more than one interior to consider try using colour coded floor plans to review your overall palette.

Orchestrating the gaze. Imagine an ideal path for the eye to follow upon first entering. How is the scene framed? How can your design help to visually prioritise the more important primary elements before moving to the secondary elements?

Framing is as simple as cropping – either in or out providing there is enough content. The aim is to reveal just the right amount of content – not too much, not too little, just enough so the ideas behind the design are expressed in this interior view – other accompanying collages can reflect remaining ideas in other nearby spaces. It should be possible to convey a sense of the design over three collages. Each spatial collage or assembled view embodies a notional two-thirds of the overall design intent.

Practice and experimentation with these approaches as part of a 'think–collage–rethink' design cycle is an important part of the design process.

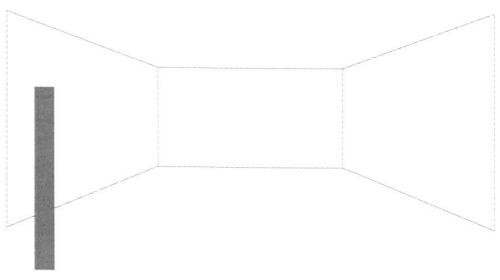

Outline Room Envelope

One method for approaching the imagination of interior space is to begin with a motif, in this case the motif is a rectangle and two trapezia. Thinking of them as flat shapes - and not the impression of an interior sometimes makes it easier to start when faced with a blank sheet.

The dashed blue horizon line here reflects the eye-level height of the darker thin rectangle - which itself represents the figure of a body and as such indicates the scale of the room.

Try experimenting with the level of the eye line and the height and width of the dark grey character to see how/if the nature of the space changes, try also to maintain the relative eye position of the blue line where it crosses the grey rectangle.

Outline room identified areas and a person

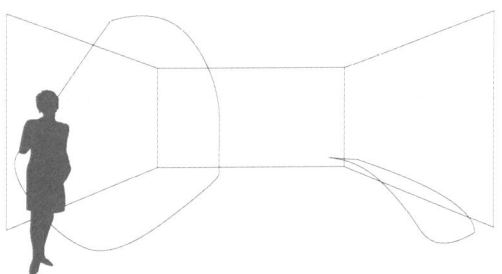

By tracing the outline of a person and scaling it to replace the dark grey rectangle it starts to become a little easier to imagine the depth and scale of an interior. The angles of the lines of the two trapezia help to define this view as a one-point perspective.

Further thoughts about the orientation of the room, its intended purpose and the nature of furniture required should help to loosely identify areas intended for different activities/furniture.

Area development

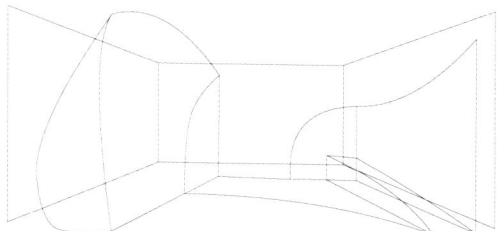

After temporarily removing the person from frame to temporarily reveal
the view the furniture previously identified regions can be expanded on
and developed further.

At this point we are still experimenting with lines and form to consider how
and which forms the new interior designed furniture might take on, whilst
also considering how these relate to the available proportion of the interior.

Moving forward, eventually surfaces become identifiable, offering the chance to flatly apply (collage) scanned material textures. At this point it's easy to get carried away, and for the purposes of experimentation and learning by all means do so. Eventually, and for the intention of resolving an interior, try to associate surfaces by role, or by common alignment and use this as a means to control the number of different textures. Typically one to three is a good number of textured elements to have in view, balanced with a similar number of different object types, and then maybe one or two people to complete a scene.

Naturally, different interior projects will ask for very different approaches, and so practice through experimentation will help develop sub-tactics for approaching new scenarios.

Rinse and repeat, less perspective

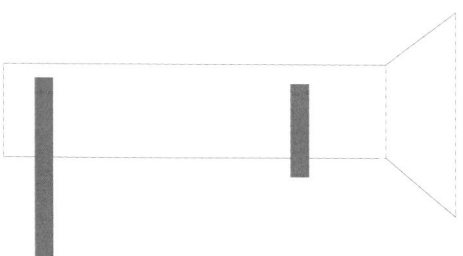

As before, this composition will use a similar process but with less perspective whilst focusing on two-dimensional elements.

Here you can see that although the two dark grey rectangles are of different actual heights, they are aligned to the same eye level, giving the impression (within the perspective view) that they are approximately the same height.

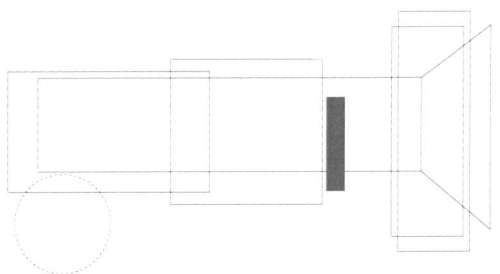

Unlike the previous experiment, the elements in play here are rectangular and faced flat with the view. As before, different positions and layering of these elements (as sketched outlines) should be considered for best fit given the purpose and available proportions of the interior.

The dotted circle here is an approximate indication of where an item of furniture might be best located.

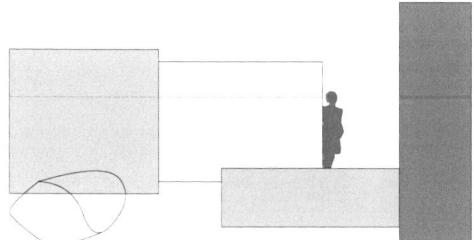

Shaded tones can work to define depth within a view. In this instance the previous range of possibilities has been edited down and developed to help move forward to the next stage.

With this process, as with sketching, we are using the view and interior composition as part of the design process – more than just a method to display an end result.

Some outlines have been removed and shapes replaced with textures,
along with sparse use of solid colours and patterns again to help convey
a sense of depth.

This is itself just a sketch of a view to illustrate how few shapes can begin
to suggest a space and imply depth. It also shows that even only three
different textures can appear visually crowded! Thus, as part of the iterative process, further editing would be useful to reduce complexity and
clarify the intended 'feel' of the room.

To reintegrate with the other design methods (sketching, plan drafting,
modelling etc) at this point a view could be translated back onto paper
in plan where it can be reviewed again to see how the interior might
balance or if there's another side to the room in need of attention.

d_Sketch model sculpting

'I work a little bit like a sculptor. When I
start, my first idea for a building is with the
material. I believe architecture is about that.
It's not about paper, it's not about forms.
It's about space and material.'
Peter Zumthor

For those of you starting out it's normal to feel overwhelmed
by the range of drawing styles and drawing types involved
in representing a project. This feeling may increase when we
appreciate that many of the different image types used to
convey a design need to have a level of parity (which is to say
that plans and perspective views are very different types of
image yet they speak of the same content).

The act of shaping an interior could be described as the
opposite of the way a stonemason or classical sculptor
might work with heavy materials to carve and shape
form. Both are fundamentally three dimensional
exercises – ultimately more formal and spatial than
graphic – though the act of interior making tends to
be more 'additive' assembling and combining different
elements, where sculpting in the classical sense tends to
be more 'subtractive' carving and removing to extract.

Effective use of the humble sketchbook and the
sketch model relies on a relaxed, part curious, mostly
experimental, playful attitude. Though much less portable

the advantage of the sketch model lies in its inherent integrity its sculpted form. Every move made, or element added, or corner removed is already consistent in plan section and perspective. Sketch models provide instant and tactile feedback. If you are considering the interior layout of a staff dining room, for example, and you have already modelled the outline dining space, as soon as you drop in a table sized piece of cardboard You'll be able to judge several things very quickly: whether it's too long; too wide or both; where it's best positioned within in the room; if it's better as one large or several smaller elements and so on. It will also show you how it works with the height of the room if maybe you want to lower the ceiling or consider a more imposing form of feature lighting. You will be given an immediate sense of whether, as a place, it feels too full or too empty and where there are opportunities to introduce different kinds of seating or other furniture or even to adjust the scope of the envelope by moving internal walls if you see fit.

To briefly return to the stone mason; the feedback loop – between material hand and head is crucial, it brings with it a level of tactile response and understanding of materiality that isn't yet fully available through computer software modelling. In striving for this kind of immediacy we can use sketch models as a springboard to carve out a sense of place. In addition, providing it has journeyed through the requisite number of iterations the resulting presentation imagery will have parity.

It takes a level of coordination to be sure elements sketched in plan align with the same elements drawn in section, whilst correlating with the perspective views. As such, to gain sketchbook confidence, consider sketching layouts from the model as plans and sections and perspectives before and after each significant set of changes within the model. Within a short time the model sketchbook and project will start to move forward in a mutually supportive way.

Sketch model corner study @1:50.
Packaging cardboard, masking tape, ruler, scissors.
Experimenting with the idea of interior landscaping, an indoor hill as a
terrain for seating. Sketch models of larger scales can help explore the
application of light and shadow in more immediate ways than sketching.

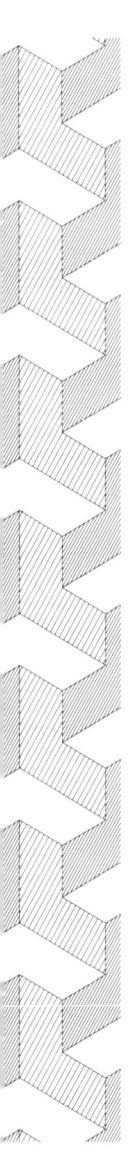

03_Coordination

How do we read environments? What route does your eye follow when you enter a new room? How, as a designer, would you go about adjusting this path? How do you make the various pieces within a room 'read' together?

An interior is composed of many elements. Even minimal designs feature components consisting of more hidden elements and workmanship than you might at first realise.

The first impression of a space will rely heavily on the relationship between these components and ultimately how they read together as a designed and intentioned environment. This is similar to first impressions presented by a well coordinated suit and tie (attire), or the opening of a piece of music – where the tempo, timbre and mood are introduced. It is in this context that we refer to coordination.

Here we can think in terms of objects material texture and colour. The first step is to recall the governing principles of the overall design approach for a project (often referred to as the 'Concept') and consider its attitude towards the four attributes listed above. It is important to be consistent from one interior to the next.

Designed interiors tend to feature very limited palettes of not more than three to four material types colours or textures. Even three colours can be difficult to appreciate, so in all cases it's easier to start with one significant colour and consider moving forward with related colour tones or material variations, this manner of reducing palettes and constraining options will lead to more focussed and coherent interior compositions.

For example, select materials with matching coloured finishes, or select variations of the same form of material such as raw, polished and mild steels combined so that walls and table tops are one type, with ceilings and doors of another type. Or similar for Oak, Ash and Birch. The darker woods could be used at floor level with lighter timbers used above at ceiling level. Once a principle is established it should be followed and only broken in exceptional circumstances where a deviation would improve the general composition of an interior and enhance the underlying approach.

Perspective and vertical lines also require coordination, this is where the object comes under review. Thought should be given to how and where the various objects can be integrated into the built form of the space or given specific compartment. An obvious example would be the fitted kitchen; in contrast to a collection of standing cupboards and disparate cooking facilities the fitted kitchen seeks to unify elements to create a composed space with consistent horizontal and vertical lines.

There are many other types of place where similar principles can be applied imagining the floor of a lounge as a landscape and coordinating furniture so that items are from a similar family of profiles (heights and depths) creating a range of objects that look and feel as though they belong together and integrate with the surrounding room.

How will you apply material, texture or colour to coordinate components? – will the flooring material match the wardrobe panelling and the headboard; or will the door finish match the table tops while other surfaces are visually muted? What is the material relationship between the components in the room, and can this relationship be defined with a strategy?

Coordinating is key for successful interior design and is a sign of a strong design 'approach'. The many combinations of things to consider can be overwhelming at first. However, intuitive strategies will develop (making it easier to approach new interior design scenarios) with practice, reflection and critique. This also becomes more manageable when the design approach is based on, and inspired by the design brief. In fact, the closer the association between design strategy and design brief (made apparent through your research and understanding) the more believable and robust the eventual design should become.

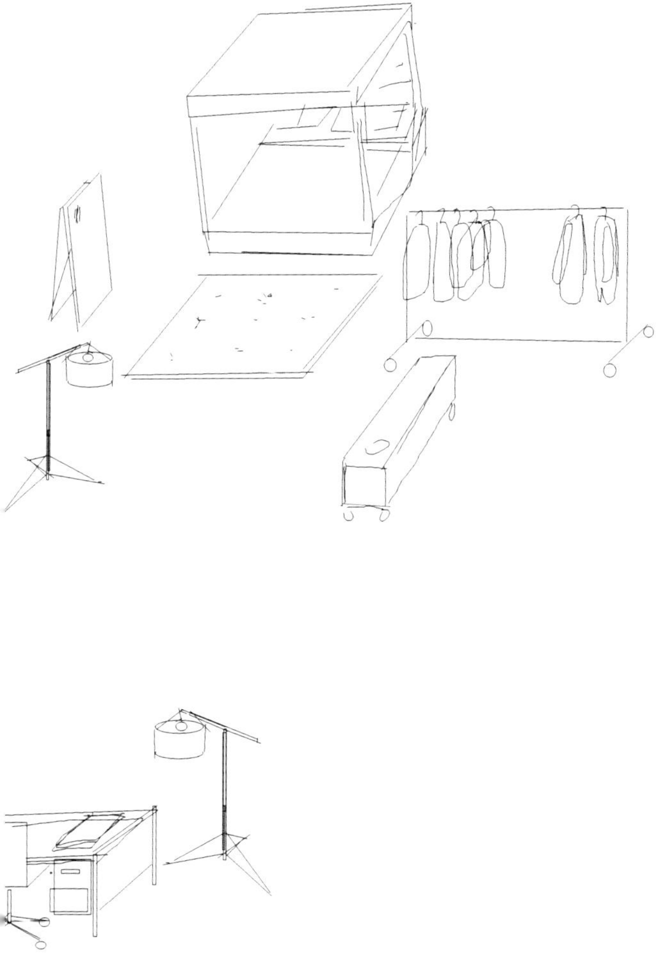

Matthis Brown 2015, Object oriented space, Digital print.
Exploration of the role furniture plays in the definition
and orientation of interior space.

The following photographs provide a sample of a small range of interior approaches, moving from furniture to fitted architectural-furniture towards textured interior environments. Each project is included for a specific point of interest. This selection is by no means exhaustive, there are many other design approaches worth seeking out. It is worth curating your own referenced digital collection of design approaches.

In this exhibition, Martino assigned himself and completed the task of making 100 chairs in 100 days, ranging from the playful to the fantastic. All parts are based on found chairs and similar components, compiled they take on the qualities of a three-dimensional collage. There is a consistency of difference which enables them to coexist as one family.

This simple but effective transformation of a desk by Torafu Architects creates its own interior environment. An effect reinforced by the inclusion of its own lighting, shelving and openable apertures which provide views on three sides. This re-imagining and expansion of the desk to a miniature room could extend to other items of furniture: the auditorium of a sofa, the landscape of a table-top and so on.

An adaptation of a former cinema building into a home by David Tapias and Nuria Salvado treats the outer structure as a shell. The rooms, platforms, stairs and dividing walls are constructed as furniture. These elements delineate spaces and places in between. Note also the continuity of timber species from the structure to the table to the window frames.

Architectural furniture: The adaptation of a library rolling book stack by 6a Architects as a display system straddles a line between furniture and installation. In addition, the usual opaque metal sheet covering these systems has been replaced with a duotone effect (varied dot size) perforated mirrored surface, superimposing reflection on transparency.

Integrated furniture here playfully re-scales the space and reshapes the room. Decreasing unit sizes create a visual texture – in contrast to the surrounding surfaces. This design by Gonzalez Haase Aas provides secondary contrast between the cartesian grid of the wall and the three-dimensional triangulated form of the product display in the foreground.

This photograph of the Rauch House layers three levels of texture: the larger hexagonal tiles with the repeating flower pattern, and the fine irregular texture of the rammed earth above.

In this project by Sigurd Lewerentz the darker foreground frames the lighter space beyond, encouraging the gaze towards it. Here light and shadow are balanced, creating atmosphere. The gravity of colour is inverted: walls and ceilings are dark while a light floor provides relief. Changing patterns provide a consistent and coordinated rhythm of line, brick and tile.

Weight in colour, pattern and texture at the Hof Residence by Studio Granda. Dark irregular hexagonal elements on the floor, with a textured higher resolution rectangular grid above, and a smooth light ceiling overhead together provide a vertical sense of gravity.

Design Team 'Assemble' and artist Simon Terrill 2015, Brutalists Playground Exhibition, Royal Institute of British Architects. This reinterpretation of a brutalist concrete playground landscape, takes the language of an external landscaped project and imagines it as a soft recycled chip foam interior.

Internal Questions

For many non-designers, when browsing furniture or exploring new places an internal personal critique might not extend beyond; 'is this nice?', 'do I like this?' or 'would it look good in the _____room?', in principle the questions are simple and the object under review is either suitable or not. However, for most designers (interior or otherwise), the nature and level of questioning often develops into a more contemplative internal dialogue.

Which formal language is being used? parametric, modernist, art nouveau, mid-century, arts and crafts? How does this design make use of colour – a tonal, contrasting, or monochrome palette? Is it made with natural materials, synthetic materials or a combination? How clear is its assembly – are its details concealed, or celebrated? Is this a visually complex piece – or simplicity itself? How does it handle the light? Will it stand quietly as part of a larger arrangement – or is it designed to be a focal point? How will these factors relate to the current and intended context?

Answers should aim to be discursive and constructive, rarely closed or final. These questions and many more should help to develop a more constructive understanding of the objects and components that combine to create our environment.

Too much of this can be a bad thing as it's very easy
for critique as a method of understanding to become a
constraint to creativity.

> 'Stupid might fail, smart doesn't even try'
> *- Diesel Campaign 2010*

In healthy moderation, curiosity about the context we find
ourselves in should only help to increase appreciation for
our environment – both natural and built and contribute
to your skill as a designer.

04_Abstraction

Be wary of form heavy motifs, and by this we mean room dominating 'look at me' forms that hold little meaning or relationship to the brief or direct experience of the user. For some designers there is a tendency to start design processes with a search for new or interesting looking shape generating exercises. For example; a brief might call for a new interior for a bakery, the design process might then respond with a study of interesting looking forms made by folding paper, or maybe an investigation of complex structures made of toothpicks, or on computer via an advanced shape generating algorithm. In this sense the process becomes technique, and the core output becomes an abstract motif. In this way, largely through design media, trend seeking practitioners have been able to compete with one another through demonstrations of ever more inventive techniques and new motifs.

However, there is an inherent abstraction in this way of thinking which often distances itself from the more interesting characteristics of the brief and the eventual design proposal. Instead of adapting this approach, try to find alternative interpretations of the design brief. This will provide opportunities to apply meaning and substance to a project that a lay client wouldn't ordinarily have thought of. The appreciation of an interior that has been carefully designed is almost always higher than for those interiors where the building's programme has been suppressed by a sweeping design statement.

All interesting interior design projects are borne out of some form of conversation. Conversation between the client and the designer, the brief and the existing building (the site), the site and the design response. In this respect where many see existing spaces as a form of constraint we see them as a chance to create something unique.

Existing buildings provide the other half of a design dialogue. Without them we would be designing from scratch, and an entire project (structure, facades, roofs) without a history or former use of its own must then be imagined. This almost inevitably weakens the resulting interior design, and thus every effort made to remove a part of an existing space or radically simplify it comes at the risk of losing sophistication in the design output, and so we look for opportunities, details, awkward corners to build around or incorporate, to ultimately enrich our work.

That said, it is important to learn about the origins and basis of different design styles positions and theories. You may disagree with some and align with others but overall it's more important to formulate an awareness of the breadth and depth of your chosen field. Eventually whilst experimenting with different projects and over the course of your education you will formulate your own theoretical arguments and positions. Arguments both for and against each of the approaches to design and design thinking that you will encounter – will only make you more informed, and ultimately make your own design output more robust when you may be required to defend your design decisions. Therefore, try not to close your mind before you've opened the book.

Looking back to the earlier chapter on understanding (02_Approaches:1); Research can provide a balanced antithesis to the constant search for new techniques. Considering the design of a new bakery, a research oriented start would involve formulating the best questions to ask about the brief, seeking out interesting details on the history of the bakery, the process of baking itself, the target clientele, the type of product made, the history of the building, the number of staff, the owner and so forth.

The greater the understanding the more appropriate the design response, the more interesting the design ideas, resulting in a design output that is likely to be inherently unique and genuinely original. Understanding how the bakery works and the different requirements of surfaces, where lighting is required or isn't needed, ranging to the more suitable furniture options and combinations, considering colour texture finishes – all adjacent to the research – may at first produce a potentially disparate array of data. This is where your design decision making begins. The data will help develop something that works, the bread, a starting point and the basis for meaning, from which further iterations can be refined into something more focused, less abstract. Further editing and a pinch of post rationalisation will help you to create the framework of an interesting project.

It is hoped that this text will serve as a preface to further study and development in this most interesting and evolving field of design.

The design world has a short attention span, and it is easy for your work to pass it by, but for the occupants your work could stand to mean something special. [1]

[1] from: "To the world you may be one person; but to one person you may be the world.", Dr. Seuss

05_The reading

Peter Zumthor: Atmospheres.
Looking at an enduring quality of place that is often
overlooked and under appreciated by many Architects
and Interior designers alike.

Junichiro Tanizaki: In praise of shadows.
In this classic (and very short read) Tanizaki argues for the
importance of darkness and contrast in interior thinking.
Shadow is described as an important and effective tool in
shaping atmosphere and defining interiors, and is a means
to emphasise adjacent brighter spaces.

Molly Bang: Picture This.
Thinking about how pictures work. A very easily digested
look at the layers used to compose an image. It doesn't take
long to read and provides another tool to help dissect any
graphic you see.

Emma Coats: Pixar Story Rules
[Tweeted series]
An abbreviated summary for story writers by a story writer
and a nice introduction to the thinking processes behind
creating a narrative structure.
http://www.pixartouchbook.com/blog/2011/5/15/pixar-
story-rules-one-version.html

John Berger: Ways of Seeing.
A contemporary polemical interpretation of art history
and contemporary culture, the book is based on a TV
series and for a long time this text was on the reading list
of every fine art student.

Clive Edwards. Interior design:
A Critical Introduction
A more thorough and in depth exploration of the profes-
sional and theoretical histories of Interior Design.

Deyan Sudjic. The Language of Things.
In this book an alternate history and theory of design is
narrated through objects, touching on both the position
of the designer and the dialogue between functional use
and aesthetic allure.

Richard Sennett. The Craftsman.
An interesting discussion on the idea and importance
of craftsmanship. In this book Sennett talks about the
idea of 'mastery', the history of the 'craftsman' and how,
as a practiced relationship between eye-and-hand, this
mentality can apply to many forms of 'craft' – from
parenting to violin making.

Patrick Nuttgens. The Story of Architecture.
Provides a glimpse into the rich cultural basis behind the
evolution of many forms of Architectural space – much of
which was developed before the existence of the Interior
designer or Architect – as professions.

Herman Hertzberger: Lessons for
students in architecture. Part 1
A must read, and useful introduction to a process of
architectural design thinking, from a structuralist point
of view, and its relationship with interior place.

Graeme Brooker, Sally Stone:
Basics Interior Architecture 01
Form and Structure
This read will take you further into the processes and
scope of interior architecture. Well structured and with
greater practical application.

Tomris Tangaz:
The Interior Design Course
A structured and comprehensive overview of methods and
techniques, also touches on the principles of practice.

Advanced:

Mary-Anne Steanne.
The Architecture of Light.
Addresses the importance and power of natural light
as a design tool and primary material for crafting space.

Colin St John Wilson.
Architectural Reflections.
A sophisticated discussion on philosophical contexts
of our built environments.

Notes:

-
-
-
-
-
-
-
-
-
-
-
-
-
-
-
-
-
-
-
-
-
-
-
-
-
-
-
-
-
-

06_A brief attempt

This chapter reflects an example set of briefs designed to build in one project over a six month programme – including studio design reviews concluding each of five parts.

In practice, studio design briefs of this nature can vary wildly between schools and tutors, depending also on studio level and tutors individual directions. As such this sample set should be understood as a loosely representative series of design tasks, written to engage at different scales of thought – from the scale of an item of furniture to the inner workings of a city block. As a sequence of slightly abstract design experiments should provide a framework upon which some of the approaches considered in the preceding text can be applied to develop your own strategies and way of working.

For this brief, Redchurch Street in East London has been selected as the general context within which to choose a site. It was chosen for its diversity of existing spaces and range of developments (new to old buildings, some developed some in need of complete refurbishment).

The planning section of most local authority websites can be a useful method for locating a potential site for this hypothetical project. Aim to find a space of approximately 80m2 (~ 750 sq ft) for eventual use in part 3 of the brief.

Many equally interesting options of similar sizes exist in most major cities, and so, should you choose to look elsewhere for the setting of your study try to identify somewhere with similar parameters and, where possible, try to reflect on the notion (discussed in 04_Abstractions) of working within existing spaces as a means to create a dialogue and counterbalance to your work.

i.   *Mapping and making*

We will begin with an object: a stool, a coat stand, or a rug. Each has a myriad of possible forms, and we would like for you to take up the mini challenge of creating something bespoke yet experimental. However, to strike a balance between function and character you will need a programme, for this we will outline a choice of:

Recording studio, or a
Citizens advice bureau, or a
Bicycle repair shop

as setting, and direction of your design brief.

Which combination of Object and Programme will you choose? Can you imagine an appropriate environment? Who works there, who visits this space and how will they interact with your object? To what extent can (or would) you embody the character of this place within the object you design? How will your experimental object interact with the chosen programme – and those who use it? Sketch and refine.

Take an explorative walk along the site to see if you can choose an existing space to remodel, one that hasn't already been 'designed' and could benefit from some attention, and walk around the block it sits within to map out the makeup of other shop types and activities of the surrounding streets.

○ **Aim:** Before embarking on larger interior projects it is important to step back and appreciate – through research – the less obvious underlying factors and potentially diverse range of elements that come together to define the character of a site. When combined with a more intimate understanding of your interior programme (the core function or purpose of your project) any resulting decisions about the form and nature of your object will be both more interesting and more believable – whilst still being experimental. This will mean thinking about a smaller component of an interior whilst also considering the much larger context of the same interior.

○ **Research:** Sketch maps of the site with outline information on how it's composed. Early notes on your understanding of the chosen programme (history of its type, how it works, what it needs, etc)

○ **Development:** Sketches thoughts and early furniture models (considering also your research) leading to a bespoke object or similar designed piece of furniture.

○ **Time:** 2.5 weeks + Review

ii.   *In which we furnish*

Now that our object is growing into a form of furniture we would like to reverse the traditional process – where furniture is selected to complement the interior. Instead, we will attempt to imagine a suitable interior for your newly developed piece and its siblings ~ other complimentary items of furniture that together make a 'collection'.

There should be up to three siblings to complete the purpose and orientation of the space in question, so for example, if you have produced a rug you might choose to compliment it with a similarly imagined bench, and a floor lamp. In the process of this we will seek further clarification of those who you imagine will use and maintain the space in which your furniture operates, their roles and backgrounds and indications of the social contexts in which they dwell.

What more does this space need to operate at its best, how many people on average will it need to accommodate, how large does it need to be, and which other support rooms are needed to assist it?

○ **Aim:** This is an introduction to sketch modelling. We would like you to create a draft model of a key room, influenced by your earlier research on the programmes needs and incorporating simplified versions of your furniture. The model will need to be imagined at a scale of 1:20 and made from easily obtained materials: corrugated cardboard, sticky tape, other packaging materials, etc.

○ **Research**: Demonstrate an understanding of the inner workings of your programme (beyond photographs and text), inhabit and sketch interior views of similar programmes from elsewhere.

○ **Development**: Sketches, 1:20 Sketch models and parts, Conversations

○ **Time**: 3.5 weeks + Review

iii.   *Associated*

As the scope increases, so too does its complexity; we find ourselves upstairs, and at the same time we are standing in an empty space next door as the owner/client of your project is looking for complimentary tenants to support her programme and help define an atmosphere. Unfortunately we can't all choose who we live with, one of the dynamics of urbanism is that even apparently odd programmes can (sometimes) find a way to cohabit where, for example, the popularity of Thai food in Pubs is part supported by the limited kitchen space of some older Pub buildings and the limited amount of kitchen space required by Thai cuisine, in fiction there is the classic tale of Sweeney Tod; the dark pairing of a Barber and a Butcher's shop, and if you investigate you'll find many more interesting examples.

This leads to the pick and mix where (just as in life) you will be allocated two programmes randomly selected from a hat. One primary the other supporting. With this combination we encourage you to find an adjacent space on Redchurch street in need of a little attention with at least two floors, and at least four interior rooms to define the area of the next part of this design project.

Primary	**Secondary**
1. hotel foyer	a. magazine shop
2. citizens advice bureau	b. painters studio
3. recording studio	c. dominoes club room
4. bicycle repair shop	d. capsule hotel
	e. private investigators office

Each of these roles should be researched separately and ideally within the context and history of this site. Your investigation should unearth interesting details and specifics that might later enable a connection between your two different interior activities – or at least support your story of how the two relate. Aim to produce not more than 500 words, hand drawings and diagrams only (NO photographs).

○ **Aim: learning to take up the challenges of different types of interior programme while contending with a more focused period of research.**

○ **Research**: Expand the depth of your knowledge of these new programmes, identifying common features and unique differences. Look into particular requirements of lighting, materials, privacy, as we would like for you to become preeminent experts on each of these types.

○ **Development**: Text, drawings, diagrams, material samples, experimental sketch modelling.

○ **Time**: 3.5 weeks + Review

iv.   *Configurations*

Imagine a scenario – the story – establishing the relationship between your two programmes. How will they coexist? Which resources will they share? How does one support the other? If you were to visit one, how would you interpret the other? How does this relationship appear in your choice of materials colour objects and lighting? More importantly: what does it feel like to be in each of these programmes and which forms of atmosphere will it aspire to?

Use your research to reinforce your story. Whilst narrating we would like you to pay special attention to the roles materials play in the framework of each programme, the roles of people involved, front of house and back of house spaces where appropriate, and the relationships between the key objects of a space and its occupants. Ultimately, these technical issues will subside and we should soon start to discuss the nature of atmosphere your combined development would like to achieve. The ability to aim for and successfully communicate a particular feeling of place within a project is an important and difficult skill. To help do so, you should always strive to expand your experience of different places, through observation and reflection.

○ Aim: We hope this exercise will culminate in at least one draft plan, two 1:20 sketch section drawings, three collaged perspectives, where possible reintroduce reconsider and collage in the materials and thoughts developed whilst making your objects in part one of this brief. This is also your chance to start exploring the idea of atmosphere and (if you wish) up to two further programme roles in discussion with your tutors.

○ Research: Buildings with mixed programmes or contrasting complimentary examples of programmes in close proximity. Separately:
The idea of atmosphere.

○ Development: Sketch section drawing, experimental collages, further material considerations.

○ Time: 4.5 weeks + Review

v.   Just a moment

Here we would like to focus on a situation where your two worlds overlap. Perhaps the relationship between the main characters of your programmes leads towards the development of a bespoke table or other new form of furniture – enacting a more sophisticated version of our first project? Or perhaps their relationship is best described through contrasts in lighting, mosaic combinations of material, specifically controlled views, and so forth?

Slightly more detailed sketch models, drawings and design investigations should lead to a focused study capable of bringing together – or at least touching upon – the various aspects of your associated programmes. This is also the largest step with the greater period of time to develop so providing you have done your research you should by now be brimming with thoughts. If not then not to worry, this is a good opportunity to discuss intentions and approaches with others, reflecting ideas through balanced dialogue will help maintain your flow.

○ **Aim:** With continued experiments in layered sketch models we would like to explore the ways in which your programmes are best portrayed. This method will quickly give way to sketch perspectives and eventually the idea of a plan but here we will focus on tutorials where your projects will be expanded and developed through references and even additional programmes – where suitable.

○ **Research:** Return to atmosphere, lighting, furniture and additional programmes where necessary.
○ **Development:** Everything.
○ **Time:** 11.5 weeks + Final Review

Research Develop Reflect

1:50 dot grid: 50cm spacings [use for tracing]

Isometric dot grid [use for tracing]

Oblique Cabinet Grid [use for tracing]

Isometric grid [use for tracing]

Notes:

-
-
-
-
-
-
-
-
-
-
-
-
-
-
-
-
-
-
-
-
-
-
-
-
-
-
-
-
-
-

Notes:

-
-
-
-
-
-
-
-
-
-
-
-
-
-
-
-
-
-
-
-
-
-
-
-
-
-
-
-
-
-

Notes:

-
-
-
-
-
-
-
-
-
-
-
-
-
-
-
-
-
-
-
-
-
-
-
-
-
-
-
-

Notes:

-
-
-
-
-
-
-
-
-
-
-
-
-
-
-
-
-
-
-
-
-
-
-
-
-

Notes:

-
-
-
-
-
-
-
-
-
-
-
-
-
-
-
-
-
-
-
-
-
-
-
-
-
-
-

Lightning Source UK Ltd.
Milton Keynes UK
UKRC02n1109180117
292309UK00011B/25

* 9 7 8 0 9 9 3 5 0 4 6 0 0 *